Woodsong
Tristram Fane Saunders

smith|doorstop

Published 2019 by Smith|Doorstop Books
The Poetry Business
Campo House,
54 Campo Lane,
Sheffield S1 2EG
www.poetrybusiness.co.uk

Copyright © Tristram Fane Saunders 2019
All Rights Reserved

ISBN 978-1-912916-70-8
Designed & Typeset by Utter
Printed by Biddles

Smith|Doorstop books are a member of Inpress: www.inpressbooks.co.uk. Distributed by NBN International, Airport Business Centre, 10 Thornbury Road Plymouth PL 6 7PP.

The Poetry Business gratefully acknowledges the support of Arts Council England.

Contents

- 5   *Argument*
- 6   Dramatis Personae | *Cast in order of appearance*
- 7   I. Duet
- 8   II. Sweeney Alone
- 9   III. Sweeney Learns the Language of the Birds
- 10 IV. Sweeney Meets a False Friend
- 11 V. Sweeney Abroad
- 14 VI. How Sweeney Ends
- 15 VII. Unwritten
- 17 VIII. Kind Earth, Cold Night
- 18 IX. Sweeney Notices a Theme
- 19 X. Eorann
- 20 *Afterword*
- 22 *Borrowed Lines*

- 24 Acknowledgements

For Jenny

'These have been some of the tales and adventures of Sweeney'
– *Buile Suibhne,* 1197 AD, closing lines

These are some of the others.

Argument

How Sweeney, king of Dal-Arie, that northeasternmost tip of Eire,
weary of his cursed state – of the fire in his mind, the loneliness,
of his transformation into a naked fluttering thing by the spite
of a vengeful preacher, and all those famous afflictions of which you are,
no doubt, aware – sought guidance in unhinged, unlikely places.

How the riddling birds of the wood sang of his past to cut through his madness;
how a future linguist taught him to unriddle the wood of his madness in song;
how a mad companion showed the future to be riddles written on wood;
how all that is written on wood is sieved by the forest's humblest creature;
how a humble written creature is saved by firewood and love.

Dramatis Personae | Cast in order of appearance

Ronan Honest cleric. Robe, sandals, large bell around neck. His church was invaded and razed by lying King Sweeney, a local landowner who tried to kill him with a spear. Saved by the bell. Prayed for a miracle. It worked: the cruel tyrant was reshaped into a form better fitting his soul.

Sweeney Honest Ulsterman. His land was invaded by Ronan Finn, a lying priest who tried to build a church on it. The cruel zealot cursed him. It worked: the kind king was turned into an insane, feathered bird-beast. Now lives in the air and sleeps on branches, his wretched clawfeet barely able to touch the ground.

All the birds of Ireland *fteewit-fwiwit-twu-chikchik-wit?*

Prof Etymologist; from *-logia* (a speaking of), *etymos* (true).

Tom or Turlygod. Four-piece suit, no shoes. Mad seer & singer. Poor poor Tom.

Woodlouse *warm small ear to the ground*

Eorann Estranged wife of strange Sweeney. Love, come home.

I. Duet

i. Ronan's Prayers

In the beginning was the Wood.
And in that Wood I built my Church.
Into that Church came Sweeney, nude.
Give it him, Father. Make him hurt.

✳

Who durst defy th' Omnipotent to arms,
Who threw his Wooden Spear to strike my Bell,
Who tore my proud Erection to the Ground,
Give it him. Lord Almighty, give him Hell.

ii. Sweeney's Song

sing a song of Sweeney
  Wood's halfpenceworth of rye
that lurching, weeping manbird
  exiled in the sky

true king of Dal-Arie
  noble mind diseased
driven from his wife and hearth
  cursed by a priest

naked, frightened, beaten
  who'll sing my song for me?
is feathered, fading Sweeney
  forgotten, finally?

II. Sweeney Alone

knows the name of every tree in Ireland;
not every kind of tree in Ireland,
every tree.

This whitethorn, where a stretch of quiet path
bends in the shape of the small of her back,
is called Eorann.

This cherry, where she counted every dot
on a tame bird-cherry ermine moth,
is called Eorann.

This willow, where he perched and called *Eorann*
till it became a sound *Eorann*
without a face

his birdmind *Eorann* only knowing Eorann
as the word for something lost
or misplaced,

III. Sweeney Learns the Language of the Birds

Utterly barking, up the wrong
tree for the season, thorn and brush
piercing his naked skin, Sweeney
halts in his howling, listens. Hush.
Caught on the wind and held, a song
fainter than breath, and cold. Sweeney
embraces the little melody, takes
to the air, and raises
his ear:

>*who killed cock robin, cracked his bell,*
>>*broke his quiet chapel?*
>*twig-boned, he flits from brook to dale*
>>*a shivering clotheless cripple*

>*who lost his lover, lost the land,*
>>*lives by his wits and has none?*
>*whose life is pith and bitter rind*
>>*and teeth too sharp for wisdom?*

And Sweeney, listening from the sky
to the lark's soft voice below, remembers
Ronan's curse, and Eorann's kiss,
Dal-Arie's hearth of golden embers.
Since every question starts with why,
and every answer comes to this,
he shrugs a gooseflesh shoulder, shakes
from his cheek, as it freezes,
a tear.

IV. Sweeney Meets a False Friend

Coughing up soot,
    Sweeney sprawls
in the grate at the foot
    of the chimney-long drop
of the hearth of a great
    etymologist. 'Hwaet,'
she begins, in a drawl.

'*Wood*: frenzied, deranged.
    Drooled from Old English *wod*,
kin to Gothic's mad *wops*
    and High German's miffed *wuot*,
bastard grandchild of Proto-
    Indo-European *wet*,
the cause of it all: to inspire.

From *wet*'s feverish (*fovere*
    not *ferventem*) fire
and its burbling pot, we get:
    the Old Irish *faith*,
meaning poet; Old English's
    wop, or song;
Old Norse's *oðr* – like *author*, you see?'

But Sweeney still can't, for the trees.

V. Sweeney Abroad

i. Flight

Another time was Sweeney so uplifted by his sorrows that his body broke the cloud line.

More than ever lost with only white below and mocking stars above unable now to will himself to earth he flew out East across the ocean to another land until fatigued by hunger Sweeney lost his grip on the hateful air and fell.

Sweeney awoke in dense bruised forest aching from his landing at a place where river slowed and curved to form a pool and yes delirious and shaking he spied the cool green watercress that curled along its lip.

He gorged himself on fistfuls of it biting till his own lips bled till yes the succulent green juices stained his cheeks and brow.

Sated for the moment Sweeney glanced towards the river in its surface saw himself twice staring twice two Sweeneys redlip greencheek wild of eye both staring back.

Who are you asked Sweeney other Sweeney answered through his lipstick and green makeup call me Tom poor Turlygod poor Tom.

ii. Poor Tom Predicts the Future

This one should be *vers libre*, I think, or something near enough, says Tom.
Sweeney does not know what to say to this, so nods.
Tom invites him in. They share his makeshift hearth.
What Sweeney knows as Albion, and Tom calls Soho,
is a city to Tom and a forest to Sweeney and this
is alright.
They spend a year there. One night,

Tom predicts he will die alone in a waterfall. I'm going there soon,
he says, and does, and dies there. And what
about me? asks Sweeney, on what he does not
yet know is the last night before Tom leaves him.
About you, I'm in two minds, says Turlygod or Tom.
So that night
Tom tells him these two poems:

iii. a future: *Sweeney Conjunctivitic*

Restive inside its amber brick,
the ancient worm begins to twitch.
Sweeney regards Odette through thick
gold-tinted spectacles. They itch.

'Life is life and death is death,'
he sang, back when he knew the tune,
tickling the yellowed keys. Stale breath.
He nictitates a yellow moon.

Luciferous, skin cold and wan,
she mimes the gesture meaning fire.
Sweeney draws two, strikes up a Swan,
lights hers – for where there's smoke, desire.

    iv. a future: *Sweeney Repentant*

Philoctetes' tired restraints
are worn and old, their leather chewed.
Feathered Sweeney counts his saints,
contemplates Our Saviour's rood

and coughs into his handkerchief.
The wrinkled neck denotes dismay
and dust, co-mingled with belief.
Sweeney knows there'll come a day

when all the damp philosophers
will frolic in the evening sun
while Pavlov feeds them phosphorus
and checks their pulses. Lesson one:

learn, and learn to live without
the lesson learnt. Invest in doubt.

                                disbelieving Sweeney rends
                                    his feathers in a rage

                              says Turlygod, how do you end?
                                 says Sweeney, turn the page

VI. How Sweeney Ends

This article may not meet our notability guidelines. Topics that do not meet this criterion are not retained as separate articles. There are, in all, three manuscripts, B (Royal Irish Academy, B iv i), 1671–4; K (Royal Irish Academy, 23 K 44), 1721-2; and L (Brussels, 3410), 1629; this is a condensed version in the hand of Michael O'Clery. The text can be dated to broadly from 1200–1500 on linguistic grounds, but John O'Donovan has asserted must have been written before 1197 when the last chieftain of [...] DEATH ACCORDING TO PROPHESY [edit] "Fly through the air like the shaft of his spear and that he might die of a spear." Suibhne [Sweeney] then returned to Ireland, to his home dominion of Glen Bocain. He visited his wife Eorann again but refused to go in the house for fear of confinement. Eorann then told him to leave, never to return, because the sight of him was an embarrassment to all. But after a while, Suibhne regained his lucidity and made his resolve to go back to Dál nAraidi [Dal-Arie], whatever judgment may befall him. St. Ronan learned of this and prayed to God to hinder Suibhne. [...] the priest instructed a parish woman employed as his cook to provide the madman with a meal (collation), in the form of daily milk. She did so by emptying milk into a hole she made with her foot in the cow dung. However, her husband (Moling's herder) be -lieved malicious hearsay about the two having a tryst, and in a fit of jealousy, thrust a spear into Suibhne while he was drinking from the hole. Thus Suibhne died [...] Cf. O'Keeffe (1913), p. xiii–xix.

VII. Unwritten

Sweeney disappearing, Sweeney out of focus.
Sweeney meeting Robinson in the old hotel.

Sweeney playing cards with Henry. Sweeney
besting Beowulf. Sweeney uncertain where he

is and who are all these people and alone again and
crumpled up in
         pain   real pain

glitching   misprinted   pixelated   leaking
eclipsed by later lesser myths   doppelgangers

namethieves: the bloodstained barber
                      the cop in a polyester suit

walls around him now long walls
a doorless corridor   astray

unhomed   lost   unwritten   nameless
not even a ghost licking milk from a puddle

of cowdung, or killed by a drunkard fate's spear
not even a punchline – he sings with his last thought of Eorann

> *the small rain down can rain,*
> *Chryst, if my love were in my arms*
> *and I in my bed again*

and as the long walls flicker, fold and disappear,
Sweeney listens for the forest's sung reply:

Song of the bear, alone.
Song of the wolf, alone.

Song of the woodlouse, she who shares
her wood-hearth with a friend, the leaves.

The louse song is a poem called kind earth, cold night.

VIII. Kind Earth, Cold Night

night	the world	to the hearth's	ours
falls	crawls	dark coals	& fills
from a great	its weight	their late	our grate
height	uncurled	warmth	with stars

IX. Sweeney Notices a Theme

Driven from his wife and hearth,
Dal-Arie's hearth of golden embers,
to the hearth of a great etymologist,
he shares his makeshift hearth,
his wood-hearth with a friend who leaves.

the hearth's dark coals, their late warmth ours
the hearth's dark coals, their late warmth ours

Sweeney places foot
    on foot on
        earth, and starts
            the long, slow
                walk
                    to Eorann's
                        heart.

X. Eorann

You know the scene. Returning from the war,
he kills a hundred suitors for her kiss.
Not that. His senses weak, her lifeless shoulders
in his arms, he fancies he can feel
her breathing quicken and the buttons twitch.
Not that. Aboard a ship, his madness lulled
by music, water and her grief. Not that.

But this. A husband, shriveled by the cold,
stooped in a doorway, mouth benumbed, too sore
to speak the words he never thought to say
and never will. He's dumb and shrunken like
a child. She seals her lips to his and waits
for something to catch light, a flame to take,
and when it does he's hers again and home.

It cannot last, and never lasts, but might
a little while. So leave it here. We'll let
this image burn across the closing eye,
consign all further pages to the fire.

Afterword

Myths are slippery things. On the first page of this pamphlet, the epic *Buile Suibhne* – or *The Madness of Sweeney* – is dated to 1197AD. This is almost certainly wrong, for reasons I'll get back to later. But regardless of when the epic about him was written, Sweeney himself is much older.

One of the first mentions of Sweeney's madness comes in an Irish law tract from around the 9th century. It's in a passage about the Battle of Moira, also called the Battle of Magh Rath – a real event, which took place in 637 – at which Domhnall, King of Ireland, killed his uppity foster-son Congal. One other story from the battle is worth knowing: the tale of the forgetful poet Cenn Fáelad, who suffered a brain injury that gave him miraculous powers of memory and invention. To this day, frustrated poets bang their heads against desks in his honour. According to the scholar J G O'Keeffe, Moira went down in history as very significant, but there's a catch. 'Amid the bewildering tangle of events in Ireland in the sixth and seventh centuries,' he writes, 'it is not easy to determine with any degree of certainty what this significance was.' Oh dear. Luckily, the medieval lawmen offer a handy recap. 'Three were the triumphs of that battle,' the tract reads. 'The defeat of Congal Claen in his falsehood by Domhnall in his truth; and Suibhne Geilt having become mad; and Cenn Fáelad's brain of forgetfulness having been taken from his head.' One of these things, they admit, is not like the others. 'Suibhne Geilt having become mad is not a reason why the battle is a triumph, but it is because of the stories and poems he left after him in Ireland.' This may be wishful thinking. *The Annals of Tigernach*, one of the earliest histories of the period, records Sweeney as having died at Moira. But there's another, better story – the story of *Buile Suibhne* – which has been lovingly mangled here.

Buile Suibhne is the third part of an epic cycle, which mixes poems and prose. Parts one and two (which we'll skip here) are *The Banquet of Dun na nGedh* and *The Battle of Magh Rath*. The cycle has been tentatively dated as 13th-15th century. It has also, however, been suggested it was written to flatter a particular chieftain, the last of Domhnall's line, who died in 1197. If so, this means it must be older, as dead patrons are less helpful to hungry poets. I'd like to think it was written in 1197, begun before the doting old chief's death, and finished just too late to be useful. Baseless guesswork, of course, but given fate's usual sense of bloody-minded irony, it's the kind of thing that might happen. A date, like Sweeney himself, plucked from the air.

Buile Suibhne has been translated lucidly by O'Keeffe, in 1913, lyrically by Seamus Heaney – as *Sweeney Astray* (1983) – and impishly by Flann O'Brien, as a digression in *At Swim-Two-Birds* (1939). 'This fellow Sweeny,' one of O'Brien's characters explains, 'argued the toss with the clergy and came off second-best at the wind-up ... The upshot is that your man becomes a bloody bird.' It's the best one-line summary I've seen. More happens in the story than that, of course, certainly more than made it into my version; Sweeney is hunted down and tamed by the long-seeking Loingsechan, has a jumping contest with an old hag, dies because of a lover's tiff between a swineherd and a cook, and is finally forgiven by St Moling, who in one medieval text is credited as the author of even earlier poetry about Sweeney.

Rather than the medieval epic, though, it's the stories Sweeney continues to leave behind that interested me. This myth seems at once half-forgotten and wholly alive, open to endless retellings, each writer holding it up to a different light.

In John Kinsella's *Wound* (2018), a 21st-century Sweeney – his home destroyed by forestry – becomes a symbol for our callous abuse of the environment. In Heaney's *Station Island* (1984), the sequence *Sweeney Redivivus* uses the character as a poetic alter-ego. Sweeney's even had the Hollywood treatment, in the US television network Starz's glossy adaptation of Neil Gaiman's novel *American Gods* (2001). Much like O'Brien (who pokes fun at Ronan's 'saint-bell of saints with sainty-saints'), Gaiman seemingly reads the story not as a tale of Christian redemption, but as a conflict between 'gray monks' and older myths.

Buile Suibhne seems to leak into anything you put near it – *King Lear*, for instance – which can lead critics astray. It's often incorrectly cited as an influence on the titular landlord of T S Eliot's verse play *Sweeney Agonistes* and his collection *Poems* (1920). Eliot's character was based on his old Boston boxing instructor, among others, the name chosen almost at random – though with perhaps a hint of Sweeney Todd. 'I happen to like the name,' he once said, 'It has a pleasant sound.' Despite much digging, I have found no evidence Eliot ever read *Buile Suibhne*. If he had wanted readers to associate his character with it, he would probably have spelled his name 'Suibhne'. I cannot find any reference to the Irish character as 'Sweeney' (Heaney's anglicised spelling) from the time when Eliot was writing *Poems*. And yet, no matter how often I stop strangers on the street to explain this to them – pausing only to brush flecks of spittle from my mouth with the sleeve of my anorak – no-one will listen. It's too late: bird-hero and bowler-hatted landlord are forever yoked together. I sometimes wonder what it would be like if the uptight poet and tattered king were to cross paths. Perhaps, somewhere altogether elsewhere, another TS Eliot is writing poems about another Sweeney.

On the surface, Sweeney is ludicrously ill-suited to the epic form: he's a naked, helpless figure whose story ends with a bathetic death-by-misunderstanding. Flapping from one inconsequential misadventure to another, with no real destination in mind, Sweeney is the anti-Odysseus. It's this that makes him so human. He makes bad choices, and suffers, and yet he keeps on singing. He is the feathered underdog in us all.

Borrowed Lines

Dramatis Personae
'Four-piece suit': 'Come to lunch. Eliot will be there in a four-piece suit.' Virginia Woolf, in a letter to Clive Bell.

Duet
'Who durst defy th' Omnipotent to arms': *Paradise Lost*, book 1, line 49.

Sweeney Learns the Language of the Birds
'who killed cock robin': The first line of the folk-song of the same name.

Sweeney Abroad
'poor Turlygod poor Tom': *King Lear*, act 2, scene 3.
'Life is life and death is death': A misquoted line from *Sweeney Agonistes*, T S Eliot (1932).

Sweeney Among the Librarians
'this poem': *Sweeney Among the Librarians*, anon., *Recursion Magazine*, issue 11/97.
'does not': *The Observer Book of Mirages*, p1197.
'yet exist': *Istence and Existence*, Apollo Jeese, act 11, scene 97.

How Sweeney Ends
A found poem adapted from the Wikipedia entry for *Buile Suibhne*.

Unwritten
'the small rain ... bed again': the last three lines of '*Westron wynde, when wilt thou blow*', a fragment of a medieval song.

Acknowledgements

'Sweeney's Song', 'Sweeney Meets a False Friend' and 'Sweeney Repentant' appeared in *The North*.

With gratitude to Katy Evans-Bush, for her sage advice on an early version of these poems, to Helena Nelson for a suggestion about Sweeney Conjunctivitic, to my editor Suzannah Evans, to Sasha Dugdale and everyone in her Poetry School workshop. I am indebted to translations of *Buile Suibhne* by J G O'Keeffe and Seamus Heaney, and offer my apologies to that work's medieval author, whose ideas I have taken wild liberties with here.